To, Mury de   ...en

wishing you all the best

in everything

love

Sudht.

X

Inside Out

Judith Rebbeck

authorHOUSE®

AuthorHouse™ UK Ltd.
500 Avebury Boulevard
Central Milton Keynes, MK9 2BE
www.authorhouse.co.uk
Phone: 08001974150

© 2009 Judith Rebbeck. All rights reserved.

No part of this book may be reproduced, stored in a retrieval system, or transmitted by any means without the written permission of the author.

First published by AuthorHouse 11/30/2009

ISBN: 978-1-4490-1239-7 (sc)

This book is printed on acid-free paper.

I dedicate my book to all my spirit guides.

CHAPTER 1.

I was delivered by the local nurse on the landing of the family home on the 7th December 1955 at 2pm, to my mother Gladys Vera and father Peter Fitzgeorge. My father an extremely hard working man toiled very long hours for the local council as a road construction driver, he was a good father who had a weak tendency around my mother whom I never really liked, she was a very cold lady never showing her true feelings, we were always detached from one another throughout my childhood.

I have no recollection of time from birth to the age of two until one day I became aware of a strong spirit guide, a very tall dark haired man wearing a long Harris Tweed coat he was an old soul who had come to guide me through the first stages of life. My mother placed my cot in her bedroom to the right of the entrance door, I can remember her poking her head around the corner of the door to check on me, when one night my guide approached me on the right side and said your mother does not love you and will never do so she was your channel to the earth plain, this was alright and made total sense to me even at this early age.

Spirit always made me feel strong and protected and having a strong mind anyway allowed me to do things my own way even if it disgusted my mother. I have a brother by the name of Paul who my mother loved dearly most often at my expense, I was not jealous but happy for him, he was receiving the love I missed out on although sometimes the constant praise he received was some what boring. My father was full of devilment and would always make me laugh with his wicked sense of humor, I did love him so much but was never allowed to get to close.

Well the time had finally come for me to start school at Weeke Infants, on my first day I could only think of myself well what's this going to be like then? and by the end of the first day when my mother collected me at 15:30 i had mixed feelings, like what was i doing here? and for what purpose, my spirit guide soon reassured me that this was the beginning of my path to life. All the other mothers would come into the playground to collect their children but my mother would wait across the road, why I thought at the time as the kind old lollypop lady would help me across the road, I remember her well always smiling and chatty. Sometimes on the way home my mother would call into the local sweet shop and get me a bag of mixed treats, she at times could be so kind, she always fed me well and kept me clean i thanked her for that. It took me some time to settle into school life but soon used my senses to choose the type of people I wanted to spend time with I was a good mixer but was always capable of detecting people's falsehoods. Listening to the teacher was boring it was far more interesting listening to other people's thoughts. Always knowing I had a gift at an early age prompted me to start my work and help anyone I could starting with a pretty little girl in my class who suffered from very bad skin problems and was under the doctor, she was always alone and sad and I wanted to make her feel safe, often talking to her when she needed to be comforted sometimes after the school bell had sounded, even then I can remember thinking I needed more time to help her but I felt reassured within that my time with her did improve her own confidence to mix with others.

Sport, what can i say, i loved PE lessons more than any other i was always determined to win and coming first was my goal.

School days came around so fast I was always fearful of what the teacher had in store that day and dinner times were my worst fear, due to the experience of a certain ginger haired dinner lady who I sensed even then disliked me. On one particular occasion she stood behind my chair and said you must eat your meat, i protested, i hate meat, she then proceeded to force me to eat it i was so sick. From that day on I dreaded going into the dinning hall at meal times, this dinner lady would always eye me up, I would try and conceal myself amongst the other eight people on my table, that hour lunch break felt like an eternity and was always pleased when it was over.

I was a popular child but not always understood by all, but this was of no importance to me, as I always knew the difference between right and wrong which being a good listener assisted me in making judgments on what was said. A fear of illness in other plagued me from an early age and I could not understand why they had to suffer I felt this was not right but as I matured I began to understand that we are returned to the earth plane to experience that suffering was part of a process to learn from and carry on into the next life, and I felt it was my duty to comfort these people the best way I could. There was so much for me to learn and with the guidance of my spirit guide I always felt safe and protected at all times.

My move to Danemark Secondary School at the age of eleven was awful I hated every day, I was becoming more aware of people's characters it was difficult to accept people around me, there were the weak souls namely bullies who prayed on the weak and defenseless who could not be strong and protect themselves from those lost souls, I felt sorry for them.

My education was really based on watching other pupils, what they looked for and there differing interests some in art, music, math's while others would get to know themselves first. I myself loved art the wonderfully exciting energies obtaining from colours. My teachers were always to busy to give up there time to answer the many questions I had so I felt very unfulfilled in lessons.

When I finally left this school at the age of fifteen I was a little lost at what to do next I always had strong thoughts on being a nun which still remain with me today but I knew I was brought back to the earth plane to work for the spirit world and had to learn and experience pain and suffering in order for me to understand others when they called me for help. So I started to look for work and finally started an apprenticeship at the local hairdressers this was not necessarily the right choice of work for me but I could not live at home for free. I remained in this job for three years before craving change again and started the search for fulfillment taking many different jobs one of which I lived in with a family running a dog kennels and cared for their two children and the dogs at the kennels. I continued to move from job to job never finding what I was looking for until I started working at a well known fashion store in Winchester high street. The experience of being surrounded by the local characters of the town made my days most enjoyable but I still kept asking myself what was the purpose of me being here, what am I going to learn, until one day I saw an interesting man walk past the shop, a voice then told me this is your soul mate it was my spirit guide, I then turned to my friend and said I am going to marry that man. Every day at lunchtime he would pass the shop sometimes running I would wave and he waved back, this went on for many weeks and the attraction grew stronger as my spirit guide worked hard for me. Then one day whilst waiting for my bus to go home a young man approached me and said my brothers walking home tonight do you like him? yes I said he then asked for my phone number so he could pass it on to his brother, things were moving so fast now I was so keen to get to know him and eagerly awaited his call. I then remembered what my grandmother once told me she said I would marry a farmers son and have two children a girl and a boy. My grandmother was a kind loving lady who I regularly visited as a young girl she was a fine medium and my mother too, how right she was this young man rang that night and we met for the first time his name was Paul Antony and he was a farmers son. I loved him from the first moment we met and after a wonderful five years together we got married on October 24th at twelve O'clock in his local village church called St Mary's in Crawley. It was a lovely sunny day and a very quiet wedding I didn't notice anyone else there we only had eyes for each other, we left the church so in love and looking forward to our life together.

We moved in to our few flat in Winchester and after a year of marriage I fell for my first child a strong and healthy baby girl born on 28th March weighing 7Lb 71/2oz we named her Sabrina Victoria, what a beautiful gift, how lucky we were that she had chosen us for her return. We remained in this flat for two years before I fell for my second child, so we moved to a house in Kingsworthy where my second child a beautiful strong and healthy boy, he was born on 21st October weighing in at exactly the same weight as my daughter, we named him Patrick Sean. I love them both unconditionally as they love me, we are a very close family and to love comes naturally.

The children started to grow and we eventually moved again to a house near where my parents lived, the children attended the local school where I also worked as a good old fashioned dinner lady. I had many jobs which I enjoyed one of which was a school for children who needed a lot of care and attention, but the one I most enjoyed was the local old people's home 5 minutes from my home I really loved listening to their stories and caring for their needs it taught me so much I really felt that my spirit guides had sent me on this path to learn about healing and spiritual work.

How I loved all the residents some were near to passing back home whilst others were still so vibrant, the only sad part being that you were never sure when you returned on duty the next day that one of the residents had passed on and returned home for their healing. It was a job of mixed emotions but as I knew where they were going it made it really easy for me to except death. I remained at this home for two years before Paul and I moved again it was a lovely house which needed a lot of work on the garden, it was one day when Paul and I were working so hard in the garden that a head appeared over the fence with a beaming smile it was an old gent by the name of Arthur, he and his wife Gwen became our best friends and having no children of their own they loved our Patrick and Sabrina who would rehearse plays for them in the garden and Gwen would play the piano. We would often go round for tea and Arthur would tell us many stories, one was so sad about his younger brother who was killed at the battle of the Somme he looked a lovely lad in the photo what a waste of young life I thought. Every day you would hear the greeting of Yoohoo coming from the other side of the fence, this inspired Patrick and Sabrina to call Arthur Mr Yoohoo every time they saw him, he loved that it made him laugh so much.

One day we made the joint decision to move again, at the time we did not know why but I followed my feelings as i felt that spirit had something planned for me. We approached an estate agent and told them we could only afford 83,000 pounds on our new home and shortly afterwards we had a call saying there is a house for sale in Chandlers Ford for 99,000 pound do we want to look at it, I replied we could not afford it and the estate agent said that the current owner was keen to move and would except an offer so we agreed between us to view the property anyway. We loved the house it was big enough for our growing family and our dogs so we contacted the agent and tried our luck by offering the 83,000 we could afford he said leave it with me. The same day the agent rang back to say they have excepted our offer I was really shocked but excited too and the agent said it was the biggest drop in price offered on a property that he had known. The whole deal went through swiftly and we were given a moving in date of Saturday 17th July 1986, on that morning we called over the fence to Arthur and Gwen to say we were off it was a sad moment but we promised to stay in touch, Arthur then said I have something I would like to share with you and gave us a framed poem which said,

To Our dear friends
It's not so very long ago
Although it seems an age
There lived a lovely family to
who we sang hello.
Across the garden fence we met
To say good morning bright
The children are delightful we

Miss with all our might
Sabrina and Patrick are their names
We never shall forget
for they are young and full of fun
we are so glad we met
we wish them well as they grow up
in there new home so nice
for they possess a lovely mum
and dad who love them more than twice
a kindly lick from all the dogs
Honey Beau, Bob all three
It must be fun if trifle hard
How will they all agree.
For lovely flowers and thoughts so kind
We offer thanks within our minds
And pray that friendship will be ours and yours
With memories bright that eye endure
Love
Arthur Taylor

How lucky we were to have such friends we though it was a tearful moment but an exciting one too as we finally locked up and left.

As soon as I entered the door of our new home I had sensed exciting things would happen here, how right I was, it was after two years being in this house that strange and scary things started to happen.

Sabrina would wake us in the night saying she could hear scraping noises from the roof space above her head it really frightened her. Paul at first looked in the roof space thinking it was mice no sigh so we sat in her room one night and the noise was very distinct as though someone was dragging something heavy across the rafters it was an eerie experience, what could we do.

It was by sheer change that one day at work I mentioned the nightly going ons to a work colleague who said I think your home is haunted and I know someone who can help and gave me the name of a lady called Christine. I called this lady the next day she sounded so lovely and caring on the phone as she listened to my story of events, she also agreed we could have a spirit who has lost its way home and needs sending to the light and would come round with a friend to assist in a house clearance. The day finally came for the clearance to take place we were all a little nervous yet curious at what was about to take place, we waited in the garden gate for these ladies to arrive Christine came through the gate first and said this is Sylvia we all hugged each other, she then caught a smell of our tobacco plants in the garden and commented what a lovely scent, they were so gorgeous that year the best we had seen and throughout our continued friendship she always remembered that scent.

We all entered the house and sat down, Christine then asked us to explain what we were experiencing in the house I answered with the dragging noises in the loft, heavy walking sounds on the landing, children talking, lights going on and off, the TV changing channels and items disappearing and turning up again days later. I also talked of my daughters fear of not being welcome in the house which made her very uncomfortable, Christine then interrupted and asked to be taken upstairs with Sylvia to the room in which the noises were taking place this I did and upon arrival at the room she asked us to leave so they could meditate. After a short while they both came back downstairs and began to explain to us what was going on, Christine started by telling us of a man who once lived in the house his name was Maurice, his sad life and his passing on the stairs at an early age, he was not ready to go over and was attracted to me as he was a single man and very jealous of Paul who as Sylvia explained he was trying to harm. Christine then requested us all to return upstairs where we all held hands in a circle and told me to request Maurice to leave this house and go to the light, whilst I was asking Maurice to go he started to push Christine around in an attempt to get to me but Christine held strong and finally Maurice went home, it was a huge feeling of relief but also a happy one to think Maurice was now back home with his family the house felt so light and refreshing as though a weight had been lifted from us.

We could not thank Christine and Sylvia enough for what they had done for us and upon leaving we hugged and promised to keep in touch which we have and still remain the best of friends today. Maurice has since returned to me in my work and said sorry for all the trouble he caused.

After the house clearance Paul and I visited the local Spiritualist Church in Eastleigh to watch Christine work, Paul has a very open mind and will listen to all topics and will not criticize people for what they believe in it's up to them he would say. During one of our visits I as given a message that the man who abused me as a child was trying to apologize, I was happy he had freed his self of the guilt, something I have learnt in life is to show forgiveness it is no use punishing yourself. I suddenly realized after several visits to the church that time was right for me to proceed on my own spiritual path and help others by doing private readings in my own home, it came so naturally to me as in a past life I also worked as a medium by the name of Annie, I lived in a caravan and people would walk across the fields to see me.

I started to do some psychic fairs to get my name known but felt it was too noisy and not private enough for my clients as you would get passers by listening to what you had to say so I decided to give this up and do sittings from home, I also visited peoples home too doing party bookings it was my way of giving them the privacy and the one to one consultation i thought they deserved. I soon gave up the party bookings as people would turn up late and treat the whole affair as a party with drink and food, not my scene and very disrespectful to the spirit world, so I now solely work from home doing sittings for those who are guided to me. One day I had a visit from a young girl she was very nervous but she soon settled down as I started to speak to her, I gave her the message that she would soon become pregnant and have twins she then burst into tears and said to me that the doctors had told her she was unable to conceive and could not have children, trust spirit I said. We finished the reading and she left with a hug at the door and said goodbye, the following week I did a reading for her mother. Six months later I had a message left on my answering machine it was from this young girls mother she was so excited my daughters having twins she said, I rang her immediately to congratulate her on her good news. She finally gave birth to a boy and girl which she brought round to see me when they were three months old they were lovely, what a responsibility I felt giving her that message that day but spirit never let me down and they always amaze me with the messages they offer, I was so excited for her and she could not thank me enough.

I have many spirit guides who assist me in my work, a man called Maurice who was a clown, I was with him in a past life as i performed in the circus as a trapeze artist I miss him dearly. Another man called Steppo a monk who has been with me in many past lives, and a man called Hemingway who my house is named after is a regular visitor a wonderful man. A recent guide to come in is a young thirteen year old boy called Applejack he lived in Victorian times and was a chimney sweep he is so black from the soot, he works with me when I do trance sittings he brings in the children that have past to spirit. He loves our four dogs he is so full of mischief as he whistles at them a typical young boy a true cockney with the words cor blimey missus often being said. I feel very humbled and yet honored that they have chosen to work with me along side my own grandmother who sits beside me she is so proud of my work. I have been working with spirit now for eighteen years and have met many interesting characters, young and old, male and female, and on many occasions I have to fight back the tears when I listen to messages being passed to me by those who once sat at my table and have since gone over. I had a dear friend called Ray who regularly came to me for a reading, he was very gifted at teaching but had a troubled soul. He lost his father and found it very difficult to cope, sadly Ray took his own life and it was when a friend of his came for a reading that Ray came to me with a message for his friend, it was very emotional moment for me but also a happy one to find Ray again.

Chapter 2.

I have been very fortunate in my work to have been contacted by many
well known personalities here are but a few.

John Lennon	Bobby Moore	Earnest Hemingway
Michael Miles	Myra Hindley	Paula Yeates
Dusty Springfield	Buddy Holly	Wilfred Brambles
Al Capone	George Formby	Anne Boleyn
Diana Spencer	Leonard Rossiter	Dr Crippen
Helen Shapero	Harry H Corbett	Acker Bilk
Steve Irwin	Tolouse Lautrec	Jill Dando

Many spirit including those of children who have crossed to the other
side by the hands of others very often make contact with me to describe
in detail how they passed over and by whose hands, but most of all for

the help to move on. Some of these spirit children are from well known publicised cases from the past, many being unsolved.

I have also been practicing psychic art in which spirit channel through me and allow me to draw my spirit friends, once as i sat in my room drawing an old friend called Mick came through, hello Mick I said its so nice to hear from you again. Mick died of a drug and alcohol overdose after he lost his parents, he found life here to hard to handle but it was reassuring that he had found his way home.

In my teenage years drugs wee always around and many of my friends who were taking them at the time are now in the spirit world they have since visited me, one lad called Andy took his own life by gassing himself with the exhaust fumes of his car, another called Terry who was run over by a car whilst under the influence of drink both very sad.

Hemingway who is with me most of the time one day channeled to me a poem,

> When still I speak your inward light
> the mirror of the soul is clear at night
> My love surrounds you like the light of day
> A perfect time to share and pray
> The touch of love that strengthens our soul
> all that's needed to see our goal
> Be brave not fear I'm always near
> Our light of love is from heaven above
> Don't work to hard save what you collect
> Be brave not fear my victory is near
> A song a sparrow a bird in the sky
> Sooner or later I will learn how to fly
> I shout from the sky I know you'll always cry
> My hand is yours you heard all the calls.

Hemingway takes a bow he is still working very hard in spirit, his fun and laughter has given both myself and those who sit with me much happiness. He had a hard life on the earth plain and although successful suffered much pain. I am very proud to have him working along side me he was a perfectionist so my standards are high to match his.

As every day dawns I look forward to what my spirit guides have in store for me, who will be knocking my door today, what messages and stories will I receive. Listening to the old souls, the way they lived, what they think of life today, the concerns for the young who binge drink, attitudes and respect for one another, many of which you have to agree with the good old days.

I have also suffered throughout my life one period was when my son was sent to a young offenders institution at the age of fifteen it drew me to wanting to help the inmates who had lost their way. I would often sit and chat to the other inmates at visiting times some of these lads were very gifted, fine artists and good story tellers we had some good laughs.

I was once approached by a lad who requested a postal reading I was more than happy to oblige him, he spoke of his main regret of his mother passing over whilst he was inside, you will be forgiven I told him she is watching over you, I am pleased to say he was released and is now doing well in the outside. On another visit it was dog sniffer day as we called it you were lined up and the dog would be walked past you if he sat down you were searched for drugs. To my horror this did actually happen to me and I was asked by the dog handler are you carrying drugs goodness me no I said he then replied do you take any herbs yes I replied then this is what the dog can smell what clever animals. It made me late for the visit and my son was concerned and asked me where I had been you would laugh if I told you I said. I have been fortunate to experience the life inmates face but sadly they do not all cope with the experience and some take their own lives, and one in my sons cell who he had to cut loose from the ceiling a very traumatic time for him this lad has since apologized through spirit to my son, he has received his healing.

Both my children will be fine mediums when the time comes; my son is the seventh son a highly gifted position, my daughter while working as a florist has made many bouquets for family funerals and they have thanked her from spirit, I am very proud of my children and inheriting my gift which they use so sensitively in the quest to help others.

One of the undertakers who worked with my daughter did the funeral of my husbands dear Nan Mary.

How proud I am to be involved in the spiritual world I guess it was all planned for me at an early age, I too worked as a florist where I met a dear lady called Mrs. Critchell who just happened to live two doors up from my husband, she is the godmother of my daughter and has remembered every one of Sabrina's birthdays a true friend to this day and well in her nineties. There are a lot of my friends and family in spirit now, my aunt Patricia who has visited me since crossing over to say I am back with my husband Reg now, he passed away many years ago. All my grand parents are in the spirit world now, I was always closer to my mothers mother who when I was young girl we visited every weekend, you were always welcomed with a lovely smile, such a warm lady a cup of tea and a piece of cake was on your lap as soon as you sat down. She was a natural medium too her birthday being two days away from my own, she was so down to earth I could talk to her about everything. There was always that smell of carbolic soap in her house, you always no when she's around the smell of carbolic in the air, she loves our car and travels with us constantly and even on a warm summers day the carbolic smell is so strong. How truly lucky I am to have my Nan watching over me her last words to me before she passed to spirit was be a good girl Judy she always called me that and although I was full of devilment I feel I have achieved this. She is so proud of my work with spirit and the help I give to others, she loves my dogs as she had had one of her own a black poodle she adored it and she has it with her now once again. She loved animals and is so proud of my work as a animal healer and I have given many people the proof they seek that their beloved pets are well on the other side and waiting to greet them on there return to spirit.

I have a deep love of all animals and find it easy to communicate on their level, as a small child I was surrounded by animal's horses which

I rode and pigs and chicken which I fed. My worst fears are snakes and spiders the sight of them really frightens me, my son told me he once killed one in his cell as it crawled up the wall the next day it was back on the wall again he has never touched one again.

My grandfather on my fathers side was a lovely man, he lived such a full life traveling the world in his work, I visited him at weekends at his home in Hamble when he worked at BP, I remember once when cutting his hair I nipped his ear with the scissors it must of hurt but he said don't worry and laughed I was so upset. I as fifteen when I last visited him and he said to me I will not see you again he was so ill but knew he was going home I was devastated and the journey home in the car was a long and lovely one. My mother said to me your quiet but I could not mention his last words to me and sure enough two days later he passed over. The one precious thing I hold with me today is the love he taught me and to be sensitive and strong as he was. My mother loved him dearly and they have much catching up to do in the spirit world.

My mother was extremely ill before passing over she was not a lucky women health wise and suffered for many years. We were not close she could not understand my gift, I would regularly pass on messages from loved ones in spirit and tell her what she was thinking it unsettled her I thought it was normal and everyone had this gift. She finally passed at the age of 76 of lung cancer she weighed a mere 5 stone. I was in the car with my daughter we were out shopping for her wedding dress when my brother rang to say she had passed over I remember feeling blank at the time she was my mother but she never allowed you to get close.

The following day I was doing a sitting for a lady when my mum appeared over my left shoulder I asked her why she was here you should be receiving your healing she was lost and had not crossed over. My friend and I sat together and helped her pass through the light, she now spends more time with me on the earth plain than she does in spirit working along side me during my healing sessions she is so proud of me now and watching over me. Mum came from a large family of ten which in those days was nothing unusual, certain subjects were not discussed in her day as they are today we are more a much more liberal society, even during my own childhood many of my questions were unanswered and in some cases avoided altogether. Mum was a very proud lady but very Victorian in many ways but I had to respect the person she was and form my own ideas on the ways of the world. I was always encouraged to join in with people of my own age participating in activities such as ballet, brownies, guides and most enjoyable of all swimming, for which I represented Winchester. I visited the local baths everyday and had an excellent instructor by the name of Mr. Collins a very dedicated man, he is in spirit now and told me to teach my daughter to swim which I did, he still helps me today in my work I am very proud of him.

I had an uncle called Charlie who we visited as a family at weekends he was a marvelous story teller and with the cockney accent they seemed so real to me. He always made me laugh, he was a think man who loved his cigars and was very strict with his own daughter called Susan. On one particular visit my mum told me that uncle Charlie was very ill with lung cancer I remembered being very frightened for him, he battled cancer for two years and on my last visit he said to me and give up those fags girl don't end up like me, a shock for someone to face up to at the young age of sixteen. Charlie finally passed to spirit at the age of fifty, he still visits me today and congratulates me for quitting the fags, and watched over my son through his troubles. His wife Trix is still here on the earth plain she is now 83 years old such a long time without my Charlie she would say don't worry I said you have so much catching up to do in the spirit world. Being cheeky I often question my spirit guides when will it be my turn to pass the reply I get is born on a Tuesday, married on a Tuesday you may even pass over on a Tuesday, a telling off there for asking but we have a joke within the family when it gets to Wednesday another week to go then.

I have learnt a lot about lung cancer from my guides when I asked them the question one day give me a challenge in my healing sessions send me someone who needs my help and sure enough a week later a lady booked an appointment for healing, I opened the door my names Lynn she said I have lung cancer and the hospital have given me three weeks to live. This was the challenge I relished and I took up this challenge immediately working on her twice that week and twice the next really long sessions and very draining for me but I did not want to let spirit down. On her third visit I asked my husband Paul who was upstairs at the time to come down and assist me as I felt she needed the extra healing energy. He is a very good healer but chooses not to apply it on others at present as he is not confident within his self yet of the abilities he possesses, I asked him to work on the stomach area while I concentrated on the upper body, so much heat was generated during that session that Lynn commented afterwards I could really feel the energy flowing into my body it was so relaxing I didn't want it to end. During Lynn's fourth visit she told me she was having a routine scan at the local hospital the next day, I told her to ring me straight after the x-rays were done with results, I sat at home feeling very anxious throughout the morning of the tests yet felt very confident inside that my guides would no let me down, when the phone finally rang I picked up to hear Lynn's voice she spoke and said the doctors told me they have the wrong results because the x-rays were clear and they can not be yours, he left her for a while before returning and saying they are yours, we both cried together like little children. I still worked on Lynn once a month until she was given the five year all clear and she still lives to this day and always thanks me.

My second case funny enough was also called Lynn a very educated lady she was a gentle sole and very spiritual, she always took away with her my guides advice, my healing guide a Chinese man once a doctor his self and experienced in the world of herbs certainly knew his stuff. Lynn and I grew together as friends and we both had a love of dogs she also had two of her own, my best friends she would say all the extra healing I need. Our sessions continued one day she would be high in spirits and the next quite low it was very exhausting. It was one evening before her next session I received a call from her I can not visit you tomorrow I am too ill to visit you can you come to my house, of course i replied but my husband Paul will have to bring me as I do not drive, I took the address and waited for Paul to come home from work. On his arrival home I said we have to visit Lynn for a healing session she is very poorly ok he said, he has been very supportive of me wonderful with my work he never complains and takes me to all my visits no matter how far or what time. I gave Paul the address and he said that's in the village next to the one I grew up in, on arriving at Lynn's we parked the car and knocked the door her husband opened it and escorted me upstairs to Lynn's room she was lying in bed I had this feeling that her husband thought she was a nuisance, he then said I am going out and left me alone with her she smiled as I entered the room I kissed her on cheek and got on with the healing session I needed that she said on completion you have earned it I replied my pleasure. I booked an appointment to visit her the following week and left, how's she doing Paul asked not good I replied poor girl I think the husband does not care about her I said I can see that Paul replied he could not get out the door quick enough after you arrived I saw him from the car. The following weeks visit soon came round and when I entered the room this time she was using oxygen to breathe and although I gave her healing I knew this was the last a vicar stood by my side throughout the entire session saying prayers. On leaving I hugged her and kissed her cheek promising to visit the next day yet knowing inside I would not. And sure enough the next morning her husband rang to say Lynn has passed over I was honored to have known this lady she was so brave, she also has visited me since her passing to thank me for my help and to say she has received her healing in spirit and doing well. I was not angry for failing to cure Lynn because your passing date is not of your choosing it was her time we can not interfere with that, you can only ease the path and comfort them on the way.

To much surprise my healing was in demand and my guides needed me again, the phone rang my names Lynn from up the road I have lung cancer can you help of course I replied and booked an appointment. I put the phone down and said to my guides that's three Lynn's all with lung cancer how strange is that. Lynn arrived at my door the next day a tiny lady but very tough she told me her husband passed over with a heart attack at 40 and she has raised a young son and daughter alone, after chatting to her I realized she was angry inside that she had cancer, she smoked heavily and I advised her to quit but she refused, I faced two challenges here the cancer and the anger and worked very hard with my guides on Lynn for over an hour that day and arranged to see her the following day. The next day arrived and I carried out the healing she was even angrier this time and knew inside she was going to pass over so on leaving we hugged and said goodbye at the door I came back in and shed a tear. Sure enough the next day a knock at the door her daughter Lucy stood in front of me crying her eyes out don't tell me I said and led her into the living room and sat her down, mum has passed she said poor Lucy she really needed help. After a while of talking she asked if she could see me after school one day of course I replied. A week had passed and Lucy finally arrived at my door we sat and she told me how she was going to lie with her Aunt, Lucy was a believer in spirit even though she was only fifteen years old, I knew she would be OK. I wished her well and gave her a hug and we said our goodbyes, spirit have taught me not to shed tears but it is really tough sometimes. After closing the door I sat for a while and talked with my guides, what a journey I have been on and how I was looking forward to the next challenge spirit would sent to me.

Paul my husband has been wonderful and a great helper for spirit, watching the dogs when I have readings keeping them quite for my friends. He has sat for hours so patient and the dogs not a sound, my eldest dog Sky a Yorkie she is thirteen and has sat in my work room since a puppy never making a sound and a great healer for people who visit, she has even smelt cancer on patients I am healing.

My other Yorkie is frightened of spirit and turns to jelly when the spirit children touch his tail he runs and hides under his blanket poor boy he just doesn't understand they mean him no harm they are playing with him. My other two dogs are Shih Tzu brothers aged three they both see spirit but choose to ignore and not join in. I have had some wonderful messages from spirit to pass on about their pets, animals can also communicate from the spirit world and through me can let their owners know they are well and remind them of the fond memories they once had and can have again. I have had dogs apologize to their owners for being run over and we laugh when they say sorry for biting them. I find animals so beautiful and they offer unconditional love not asking for it in return.

I once did a sitting for a lady and brought through her white parakeet he had a cheeky look in his eye and wanted to be reminded to his owner. He talked very well I said when he was with you and kept repeating her name, I also had to tell her he had learnt to say He He He in spirit, is he winding me up she said I used to blow on his beak when he would not stop talking to annoy him, yes I replied he was having a laugh at you now, he left her with the message who's a clever boy then to reassure her he was OK on the other side and having fun.

I have been able to bring much comfort to those who still grieve for their long lost pets and such a joy to see their faces when they are reunited with them during a sitting. Many people I see have used their pets as support when they have lost a loved one and found this the only way to cope, even the birds that visit our gardens can bring healing to those people on there own who watch them as a form of therapy. I myself have a sparrow hawk that regularly visits looking for food, I was once surprised to see a large Heron sat on the fence overlooking the pond hoping to catch a meal, I have been blessed as a sensitive to hear and feel what these beautiful animals are thinking.

The many questions asked about myself by clients.

Do I feel different as a person ? the answer is yes I have always felt different.

Does your gift frighten you? No I reply it give me happiness and joy

Do you see and hear spirit? Yes to both is my answer since a small child.

Do you receive bad messages? I do, not all news is necessary good and we have to deal with both as a medium.

Do I get premonitions? I do is my answer I saw the twin towers go up well before the actual event happened.

Do you see peoples illnesses before they arrive, unfortunately I do I reply.

Do I fear crossing over? Not at all I reply I will be returning home to see long lost loved ones again.

Has your mind ever gone blank during a sitting? No thank goodness.

Have you any idea of your past lives and who you wee? I have had many lives some good some bad and how I passed.

Do I have any fears? Yes I reply heights is one as in a past life I leapt from rocks to take my own life. Spiders and knives are two others I was stabbed in a past life.

Do you get lonely? Never there are plenty of spirit friends coming through to me.

Have you people around you all the time? No I love time to myself to meditate with my guides and to cleanse the mind and restore the lost energies within myself.

Do you miss any one in spirit? Of course there are many both human and animal.

Have you been a medium in a past life? Yes in one life as a clown in a circus with my sole mate Maurice.

Have you any regrets? No not really life is a journey all ready mapped out for you when you come on to the earth plain.

Do you have any wishes? These are endless, to one day visit my spirit guides house in America, to swim with dolphins, to se both my children living there own dreams and also working for spirit when its my time to go home, to write many books to educate others about spirit.

Have you any disciplines? Yes, I do not smoke or drink and I eat no meat and exercise daily, to keep my mind clear for spirit.

Are you religious? Depends what you call religious I do not attend church, I do not preach my beliefs to others, I do pray for those who need help, I will help anyone who asks. I strongly believe you can only answer to your self for your actions.

What do you hate? Many things, bullying, bad tempers they show a sign of weakness, stealing, cruelty to all creatures, adultery and lying.

What are you good at? Sport including swimming, ballet, cycling, running but not so fast now, knitting, sewing and not giving up in something I truly believe in.

Have you any weaknesses? Oh yes working to hard, coffee, and being to hard on myself.

Had you any career wishes? I wanted to be a nun at a younger age, to work with animals what a joy, to work in Chinese medicine and specialize in herbs a great hobby of mine one in which I have gained much knowledge.

Do you believe in abortion? No I do not you are stopping a soul that wishes to return to the earth plain, but for reasons of health is OK.

Do you get cross during sittings? Never I am taught to listen and no judge and to try and direct and guide them on the right path, only they themselves can then decide on what's been given and which path to choose.

Is there anyone who would really love to do a reading for? Many like Patrick Swayze, Tina Turner and Jamie Oliver to name three, because I admire there bubbly characters so alive and full of fun.

Have you done sittings for people who refuse your help? Yes some people either refuse the help or are just not ready at this time to accept it.

Have you had a good reading done for yourself? Yes to both by men they seem to link in with me better, Psychic Artists link well with me too.

Do you have regular readings done? No only when I feel the need as I use my guides for advice.

What has been your best connection with spirit? One time whilst in bed two of my spirit guides appeared leant over me to within inches from my face and both smiled Wow I thought and said thank you to them.

Have you experienced Astral travel? Yes I have been back to visit my spirit family on many occasions.

Do you see Auras? Yes around people all the time they tell me so much about that person.

What do you enjoy more doing a reading or healing? I have no preference both are for spirit, one heals the mind the other the body.

When will you give up your work? I will continue for as long as spirit require my services.

Are some of your clients frightened? Yes but I soon put them at east telling them I am no different to them but have a gift I want to share, To make them laugh i sometimes tell them you should be more frightened of my Yorkshire Terrier he bites your feet given the chance. Of course the dogs are out of sight as some people fear them and I respect that.

Do you have house rules? Yes like everyone has, no smoking, the removal of shoes when entering and no swearing.

Do you receive gifts? I do lovely cards, bunches of flowers, letters and phone calls thanking me for my help I treasure them all.

Do you respect other religions? All of them it is the individuals right to choose in what they wish to believe.

What's your favorite part of the UK? With out a doubt Yorkshire the countryside is beautiful and the people so friendly.

Where would you love to visit? Scotland and America hopefully one day.

Have you performed Trance? Yes with the help of my guide Apple Jack

Has a celebrity visited you? Yes but I treat them the same as anyone else.

Have you been approached for help by the Police? I have on occasion but I can not say which ones.

Do you have spirit in the house? All the time and many.

Do bad spirit visit you? I have but they are told to move on they are not wanted here.

Are items brought to readings? Yes photos and items of jewelry on many occasions which I hold and receive many vibes from, sometimes people have removed their wedding rings to test me out how silly.

Have you worked with another medium? No never I have been asked but refused I love to work in my own way.

Have you achieved all in your spirit work? Not at all I have so much more to learn and many people still to help.

What will you do if you finally retire? Travel with my husband.

Do you se your husbands guides? Of course he has a Massai guide who is very tall and I once bumped into one night on my way to the bathroom.

Do you see spirit when you first awake? Always they watch over us whilst we sleep.

The questions asked of me are endless I could mention many more.

Once when on holiday in a cottage in Eastbourne I felt the presence of a lady she had passed over in the cottage before her husband. He had remarried and living on in the cottage with his new partner before moving away, she was a very angry lady and gave us no peace all week, our dog spent the whole week shaking and would not sleep in the bedroom as usual.

There was also present a little girl and one day from no where a teddy was thrown towards my dog she wanted him to have it.

We have stayed in many cottages and felt spirit in them all, another was an old converted railway station near Scarbrough not very quiet at all the old porters and ticket collectors spirits still walking through as though it was still the station. Another cottage we stayed at was called the old nick in Derbyshire which was very apt as it was the old policeman's house with its own cell attached, this was now a bathroom with the original cell door still in use, a very lively house I must say with some troublesome spirit who did not want you there, but we learn to cope and respect them for wishing to remain in this place.

I am asked many times about what my husband thinks about my work, does he ask lots of questions, no is the answer he respects my work and that is why he was chosen to be with me, he knows the amount of energy I use in my work and would not wish to drain me any further, he is very open minded and knows spirit are around but remains quite casual. I will sometimes pass on messages to him when they are given to me from his loved ones in spirit. He works as an electrical supervisor which is quite appropriate sometimes when the lights are turned on and off by spirit most of the time at night left on, doors opening and shutting and the Tv on late at night and quite loud, knocks on the ceiling and footsteps on the stairs happen regularly but we have adjusted to all this and it has become a routine and sometimes quite funny but in no way is it frightening it is spirits way of letting you know they are there.

Readings for my clients.

A lady who I will call Mrs. S came to me I sat her down and began by first relaxing her she was so nervous, the first spirit to appear by my side was her grand mother hand on hips she asked me to say to her with those wide hips you are going to give birth my girl and laughed, Mrs. S burst into tears, she always said that to me, fine I said you can now stop worrying and look forward to the birth, again she burst into tears I am not pregnant i have been trying for a baby for five years without success, believe spirit I replied you are and I suggest you get a test done right away. Later that evening a phone call from a delighted Mrs. S confirmed spirit was right she was expecting we both shed tears and she thanked me, my pleasure I said.

Miss C came to me she was so tense we sat down and chatted for a while and I sensed she was a frightened and confused young lady and in a great deal of emotional distress. I started by telling her she had four children by four different fathers I have she said, I also told her you are pregnant again and its not you boyfriends I am she replied and my boyfriend is in prison I am frightened he will kill me if he finds out. You have decided to terminate the pregnancy haven't you I said, yes she replied my guide jumped in and said its her fourth termination oh dear I said no wonder you're so confused and emotional I can not influence your decision as its not spirits way, but you must think of your health it can be so dangerous I know she replied. You must make a choice and that choice is one that only you are happy with, she was still determined to carry on with the termination it confused me as to why she was not listening to my advice, but I realized she could not change as she had brought her past life into her current one. You learn as a medium that you can not help everyone only those that are prepared to listen and believe, I finished the sitting and we hugged at the door I said god bless and good luck for all you look for in this life, I came inside and thought to myself poor girl she really needed a motherly figure to hug and hoped she would get it right in the next life.

Mr. R came to see me a very tall man, we chatted for 15 minutes and I soon picked upon his sense of humor and he loved to talk he wanted to tell me everything so I quickly stopped him and said you will spoil any surprises that spirit have in store for you, I smiled at him which put him at ease and we started I said to him you do martial arts and work with young children, I do he replied, he was what I call a gentle giant with a heart of kindness.

He was a troubled sole, he had diabetes and regularly injected his self, he was ambitious and wanted to progress with his martial arts even though he held a black belt. I then told him you smoke the weed don't you yes he replied, you must stop as it will spoil your aims in life. The reading went well and we parted at the door with the usual hug and a thank you. It was two weeks later that I received another call from Mr. R he wanted another reading so soon I said and I only agreed as he sounded anxious so I agreed we sat and he said he was having girlfriend troubles my spirit guides worked really hard with Mr. R that day and he finally left with a smile, I knew deep down I would see him again and sure enough a month later my phone rang and a voice said do you remember me of course I replied you are Mr. R, I am desperate to see you again and we arranged a date.

The day arrived and as he sat at my table he burst into tears and said my father has passed over he hanged his self and it was I who found him, poor sole I thought, I spent the next two hours consoling him and helping him find the inner strength to survive the grief he felt for his loss, it was an energy sapping reading for me, but as he left I could sense he would not be with us on the earth plain very long, and within a month a friend of his called me Mr. R has taken his own life he could not cope without his dear father and friend, what could you say it was a pleasure knowing him and I will always remember that sense of humor, but I knew he was reunited with his father now in spirit which he has confirmed to me when he came to me and said I am happy now and thank you for all you have done, his sense of humor is still with him we smiled and I said god bless my friend.

It was the start of a new week and my next sitting was a Mr. M at 10 o'clock and he arrived right on time I opened the door to him he looked so empty and lost. We sat at the table and began you have a son in spirit by the name of Stephen I said he looked surprised and said yes, I continued by saying he was killed in a motor cycle accident on an A road that's correct he replied, Stephen then started to explain the sequences of events surrounding his death, the road was damp dad and I tried to avoid a dog and that ran in front of me and hit an oncoming white car, I remember leaving my body and seeing it at the side of the road, he then said sorry dad, Mr. M by this point was quite emotional and shedding tears, we continued with Stephen reminiscing about times spent with his father and family and even told his father about his bedroom being left exactly the same as the day he passed, it is Mr. M replied its our shrine to him. Stephen then said goodbye dad I am going to see my friend, Mr. M then confirmed the driver of the white car saw Stephen swerve but did not see the dog. My guides and Stephen did all they could to give Mr. M closure but on leaving I knew this had not been achieved due to the not knowing that a dog was the cause, I said my goodbyes yet knew I would see him again. Sure enough a few months later Mr. M appeared at my door we started the sitting and it was his son Stephen who came through again a huge smile appeared on Mr. M's face he loved talking to Stephen. Stephen was full of fun and teased his father by telling him he had a better motor cycle than him in spirit, this made Mr. M laugh even louder, in fact throughout the reading we laughed constantly at Stephens jokes, Stephen then said its good to see to laugh dad its been such a long time, but you must now move on and let me go I am OK, there was a sigh of relief in Mr. M's face, Stephen pulled back and left his love to his dad. I think Mr. M has moved on a little and across the space of time will regain his life fully but always have fond memories of his son, he left the house and said thank you for all you have done, my pleasure I replied.

My phone rang and I answered to hear a squeaky voice on the other end, are you Judith the medium they asked, yes I am said, can I make an appointment to see you, of course and we fixed a date. Mrs. L finally arrived for her sitting and we sat at my table and chatted for a while as I always like to do as it puts them at ease. During our chat Mrs. L said can you not tape the reading please she looked terrified, I will always carry out your wishes I replied. Mrs. L was a tiny lady with a sweet and yet timid character she had a strong pat life still with her almost Chinese looking. I started the reading by asking her the question why are you allowing yourself to be controlled by your husband my dear you are living a life of fear and turmoil. My guides then said your husband has a infatuation with Thailand hasn't he and he make regular visits he does she replied, my darling I said I don't need to tell you because I think you already know this he has been betraying you and with several women, Mrs. L then burst into tears and said will he ever stop being unfaithful to me, I carefully replied, I don't want to be the bearer of bad news dear but I am being told that as long as you allow this to continue he will not stop. I then said to her this had been going on for a number of years my love hasn't it, yes she said, why do you allow yourself to be hurt in this way you are such a lovely person and because of this he abuses you knowing you will not complain, I know she replied but then said the worst thing as I want to take an Aids test just in case, I haven't got it have I she asked, lets wait and see I replied knowing deep down she had contracted it but felt it was not the right time to tell her, it is sometimes a most difficult choice to make as a medium to decide how much information you should divulge to your client, especially when they refuse to help themselves. We parted that day with a big hug but I knew she would be contacting me very soon and sure enough some months later I received a phone call from Mrs. L to say the test has come back positive, I am so very sorry I said it's a hard lesson for you to learn of life and one you must now suffer for you poor thing, I felt really helpless and could only offer her moral support. I am so stupid she replied I let my heart rule my head, I wished her all the best for the future and deep down I thought what a price to pay for someone else's actions and hoped her next life would be a more rewarding one.

It was ten o'clock on a Friday morning when Mrs. J came for her sitting I opened the door to this lovely lady with a warmly smile, I have been trying to pluck up the courage for two years to come and see you Judith she said, my goodness dear I replied well I am so glad you're here now so please take a seat so we can begin. I immediately felt that this sitting was going to be a good one and I opened up to tell her you work in a care home for the elderly don't you, I do she said, how lucky they are to have you I replied, well thanks she said, I have the whole of the nursing home here in spirit waving at you and saying thank you for all the love and consideration you gave to them. An elderly lady then stepped forward she laughed so much she at first could not talk and finally she spoke laughing my names Lily she said, Mrs. J replied I remember her we had so many laughs together I could not get anything done. Lily spoke again do you remember one day when you tried to dress me I was so ticklish it took ages, I do Mrs. J replied. Lily was not a lady to mince her words I am sorry about all the flatulence I seemed to have we all burst out laughing, do you remember the day I leaned forward to stop my biscuit falling into my cup of tea and my false teeth fell into the cup instead, more laughs by us all, Lily seemed to make her own fun and Mrs. J said to me I have never laughed so much since those days and thanked Lily for coming through to say hello and bringing back such memories, Lily then said goodbye and disappeared. The next spirit to come through was that of her real father which he repeated twice i felt he needed to underline this fact my love I said, Mrs. J's eyes filled with tears and she reached for the tissues I always kept at my table. Your mother has deceived you all these years I said, she has been married three times, Mrs. J then said to me my mother never told me this and led me to believe that the man she was married to was my father. I then said your real father has been trying to contact you for years but your mother moved away and changed her name, he had tears in his eyes as he said I have always loved you and I will always watch over you I am so proud of how you have turned out. I then said to Mrs. J you have found some information out for yourself haven't you, the fact that your brothers and sisters you were told were of the same blood are not they are from different fathers, I certainly did she replied I can never trust what my mother says again. I then had a lady appear to my side I am your grandmother she said I fell so responsible for my daughters behavior she was always hard work for me I would have loved to have you as my own daughter we would have had so much fun and shared so much love, Mrs. J was so happy having a spirit family step forward and showing the love they had for her it made her realize love for the first time in her life. Mrs. J was using her work for the elderly to receive the love her mother refused to give and to return her love back to them. I finished the sitting and we sat and chatted a bit longer, I can not thank your spirit guides enough she said so much has come through and I feel I can now put closure on the past and look forward to my life ahead, its my pleasure I replied, we hugged and I wished her well, she then left and walked up the drive with a more noticeable spring in her step than the one she arrived with, I do so love my work when you can assist people so much and help them move on.

It was an evening appointment and Mrs. W turned up at my door at 7 o'clock sharp we said our hellos and I led her through into my room and sat her down. We began the reading and a young lad came through to me and stood along side Mrs. W he was a very handsome young man with dark hair my name is Steven he said this caused Mrs. W to raise her hands to her face and she burst into tears, I reached out to comfort her. Steven tells me he is your son, she nodded yes he tells me he is sorry he left you with no explanation for his passing over, he continued to explain that six months before he took his own life he knew he had to return home and could not remain on the earth plain. I was like a closed book he said not allowing any one into my life including his mother Mrs. W agreed with a nod, I never meant to hurt you but I needed to return home. Steven then said I am with my friend who was killed two months ago and we are laughing together, I told Mrs. W you have a son who is full of fun, give us a fag mum he said my mate could do with one, this made Ms. W laugh and say he always said that to me he was a one. Steven then said mum you still have my trainers in the same place I left them and my sister still has a lock of my hair, that's right Mrs. W replied, don't worry mum he then said I am having fun here and will always be with you. He then wanted his mum to remind him to his friend Martin, I will she said, Steven then said I must go now and look after that photo of me you always carry in your purse he said and he left. The reading for Mrs. W lasted for two hours and as she got up she pulled the photo from her purse to show to me, this is Steven she said I find every day so hard to bear Judith but I now feel closer to him and will try to move on knowing that he is happy, he can have all my fags she said which made us both laugh, he sounds like my son I said the trouble for him is I don't smoke. Mrs. W then said to me I would hate to be a medium, what is that I replied, well to listen to other peoples pain and anguish, not at all I replied, it's a joy to work with spirit and being able to reunite people with loved ones its so rewarding, to see the relief on their faces and the upliftment it brings them makes it all worth while. We hugged at the door as Mrs. W left thank you Judith you have really helped me today I feel so much better, my pleasure dear I replied and she went on her way, I thought to myself a lot of healing has taken place today and how pleased I was to be a service to spirit.

The Christmas break arrived and seemed to go on for ever to me as I have an appetite for my work and feel unfulfilled if I am not working for spirit. The cold snap stopped and we were back to the rain January was here, my first reading of the year arrived a young lady called Sarah who I had seen once before she rang the door bell and I opened the door hello Judith she said with a smile, come on in Sarah its nice to see you again and I led her through to my room, please sit down and we then chatted for a while before I had my first visitor. Sarah I have a gentleman here he tells me he was forty years old when he passed to spirit and he drowned in a lake whilst at a pop concert. He wants you to let his wife and two children know that he is OK, he is saying my passing was an accident he slipped down a bank into the water and wants his wife and family to have closure please tell them I am still with them. He also remembers that he was found in the water by a man, and he is saying thank you Sarah for passing on this message I owe you one but I must leave now happy that you will do what I asked of you and leave you my love.

Sarah then spoke I was only with his wife yesterday how strange is that but I promise to pass on his message.

Sarah's grandmother from her mothers side then came in and stood by my side holding pink roses in her hands, these for Sarah she said you should have been my daughter, this made Sarah cry and say I loved my grandmother dearly. Your grandmother is telling me she was listening to you and your husband yesterday talking about purchasing some chicken, your right Sarah replied we are buying some next week. Your grandmother wants you to say hello to your son and daughter for her and to stop thinking to yourself that you're a bad mother, you are doing what is best for your children and no one can fault you for that, she is so proud of you. Out came the tissue box again as Sarah cried. her grandmother then said Sarah please get a check up done you have a punctured lung from that car crash you had, she could be right Sarah said after the accident I had breathing problems but no one checked and I just ignored the problem. I always feel uneasy passing on these types of messages and only do so in the knowledge that my spirit guides are always precise in what they wish to pass on. Her grandmother then left leaving her love. Sarah i said you have a new spirit guide with you and she is here to help you in your work as a designer, she is telling me that you are very gifted in what you do and wants to help you progress to the next level. She tells me you have a piano in the lounge which she has tested for herself and laughed loudly, your daughter is a fine pianist she is saying please encourage her she will do well as she is strong minded like yourself hence you tend to clash a lot, so get to know each other better she is telling me. Your son she says is very unique I like him he has a private mind, he stores what he collects and only parts with what he needs to, a very wise soul and often misunderstood but this bears no importance to him, he will do well in his life and not waste any chances that come his way. Your husband has just lost his job hasn't he, yes Sarah replied, spirit are telling me they have something in mind for him and when the times right they will let him know. Your husband is not open to spirit is he, not at all Sarah said, spirit are telling me to use this special time that they have given you to learn more about each other and the reasons this time has been allotted to you. I finished the sitting and Sarah said to me, I really did not know what to expect when I came here today but am so glad I did life's been a little difficult for me lately yet I now feel more positive and peaceful as though a cloud has been lifted from my mind, many thanks to you and your spirit guides

Judith, my please Sarah and love to your family, we hugged and Sarah left.

The sun was shining brightly when Miss V came to my door she has been to me on a number of occasions a very likable character and easy to work with. Miss V is a very talented photographer but never gives herself the credit she deserves as she strives for perfection and is her own critic. I always find in line of work that the gifted ones are always striving for more and rarely given themselves the credit they deserve.

I opened the reading by telling Miss V you have a saucy feeling inside, I have she replied with a cheeky grin, you have your eyes set on a young lady who competes in the triathlon events, I do she answered, how funny this lady has led you a race in a past life and you still haven't caught her yet. She has her hands on her hips a real character, will I catch her asked Miss V, oh yes I replied she is telling me she is tired of running and going to stop to make it easier for you to catch her as you are not a good runner yourself. This lady is going to open herself up to you to allow you to express your feelings for her.

I have your father here I said, I expect he's ashamed of me Miss V replied, on the contrary I replied he only wishes for your happiness and is very proud of your work, your dad was good at giving advise to everyone wasn't he, he was answered Miss V, I loved my dad dearly she said, I know that's why he has come through to see you, he wants you to pursue more into your photography work and he tells me you will move in with your lady friend and things will be fine. He tells me you will buy a house in Brighton together and sends his love and says goodbye.

We finished the reading there and Miss V said thank you and left yet I knew inside I would hear from her again and sure enough two weeks later I received a postcard from her saying having a lovely time in Brighton with my lady friend and looking at houses together, many thanks Judith. The front of the postcard was most apt two ladies walking in the sunshine with their arms around each others waists, this made me smile so lovely to see people happy and in love, that's why I love working with spirit to give a chance to improve there lives.

Mrs. N and her daughter arrived for their ten o'clock appointment I led through to my work room and sat them down, the reading was for Mrs. N but she always brings her daughter with her.

I opened by saying I have your husband here to see you, we were hoping he would come through they said, he is telling me you are going into hospital in three months time for a hip operation and you are unsure whether to proceed, that's correct replied Mrs. N its been bothering me for ages. He is telling you to go ahead with it there will be no problems at all and you will feel a lot better, he then turned to his daughter and said thank you for taking care of your mother. You will visit the Great Wall of China this year he told her its spirits treat to you for putting others in front of yourself, you are a kind and loving soul, he is putting his hand on your left knee to heal it for you, I have just had an operation on that she said, well there you are I replied spirit always know. Your husband has just brought in with him Smoky the cat, a blue budgie, two black and white rabbits and a jack Russell, this made them both laugh then cry, I joked by telling them he wont have time to get up to any mischief with that lot will he, and we all laughed, he then said his goodbyes and sent them his love. Mrs. N i said I now have your grandmother here she is so proud that you wear her ring she says it took her a while to wear it herself, a lovely smile appeared on Mrs. N face as she held her hand up to show it to me, its gorgeous I said to her. She then spoke of the good old days how lovely it was and the love and respect people had for each other not like now she said people to busy to even say hello always in a hurry to go some where, they don't even know their neighbours in the same street any more, not like us she said we knew everyone, we all had to agree on that one so true it is. She said goodbye my loves and departed. I was exhausted by now and closed down the sitting and wished them both a fond farewell as they left.

I returned to my room to sit and close down my mind by thanking spirit as I always do and joked with them see you again same time same place then, working with spirit is a huge responsibility and I am so proud to have been chosen to work alongside them. I have made a promise to my guides to always achieve my best and assist anyone who seeks it from me.

I was looking forward to my evening appointment with Mr. and Mrs. K, they arrived on time and knocked my door, I opened it to see two sad faces in front of me and knew I would need all my guides help to assist them both. I sat them down at my table and made them comfortable, I opened the reading and said come on mum and dad I have been worried about you both, I am so sorry to let you down mum and dad I made a mistake. Your son is here and bring with him his love for you both, he tells me he was over seas with his mate when he had an accident on his motorcycle whilst racing each other. There were tears from his mum and dad as I continued with the messages, he was quite a character your son wasn't he, he led his life to the full that's how he liked it. He is joking with you now dad and asking if you have a suit he can borrow, his dad burst out in laughter and said he always borrowed my suits. He also is telling me he was having so much fun with his mate at the time of the accident, say hello to my friend and my sister for me he says. I think your new car is cool dad I have been with you in it, he tells me you recently changed his head stone and thanks you for that. His birthday is in June he tells me and can he have a new bike dad but make it a cool one there were tears and laughter at this point, quite a chatter box your son, he never stopped talking Judith they said. I've got to tell you that your son goes with you in the van and he says turn the music up dad, I will be replied. I continued the reading, spirit had so much to offer this lovely family giving them much relief. As we parted company Mr. and Mrs. K could not thank me enough and said to me we can now smile again knowing our son is OK, they walked up my drive six inches taller. Its occasions like this that makes my work so enjoyable and rewarding to think I can make a difference to peoples lives and to help them move forward, thank you spirit for your help.

UFO Phenomenon.

For those of you that are skeptic and doubt the existence you should look at all the evidence put before you, here is my experience choose to believe it or not.

When my daughter Sabrina was ten years old she ran into our bedroom and woke me up, mummy she said come and look at this as she grabbed my hand and led me into her room. She had a large double patio type door in her room which led onto a flat roof and overlooked the gardens of other houses, as we lived on top of a hill we could see for miles around, look she said and in the distance I saw three bright lights beaming down it looked as though they were searching for something, it hovered for a while then sped off in an upward direction and out of sight. My daughter and I were so excited yet frightened at the same time at seeing such a wonderful sight, and we both reassured ourselves that this was real and not a figment of our imagination, all this was confirmed the next day when Margaret whose garden it hovered over said to us did you see that ufo last night and of course we answered yes we did, I am so glad she said that someone else has seen it.

Later that night as I slept I was taken from my bed by them, not sure what they needed me for maybe my knowledge as a medium who knows, but I remember being willing to go along. I remember standing on the platform to the entrance of their craft with one of them holding my hand they were very friendly and meant me know harm, it was a most beautiful experience for me. I really can not remember much else that went on that night it was as though my memory had been wiped clean but I do remember they shared only their love with me, and the not wanting to return home but was told by a male alien I must. This experience still lingers with me today and i have never doubted their existence even from early childhood I would search the skies looking for them, and even now I find myself on some nights looking up at the stars and wondering if they will ever return again or have they got what they wanted from me already.

Animal Beauty.

I have a lot of knowledge of our animal friends and share a great love for the animal kingdom, in fact many of my clients often say to me Judith animals are much more beautiful than humans. In fact when people have hurt in their lives their pets are the first they turn to for help to pick up the pieces and in many cases to give them the courage to carry on living, a pets love is unconditional and a warm welcome is always given to you no matter what mood you may be in. I have experienced many stories over the years from clients who say their animals have made them smile again, in fact I even use one of my own dogs to welcome people in she has such a good healing nature and they all love her, it also of course puts them at ease for the sitting. The many stories I have heard from my clients who have had a dog for all of its life then when the dog reaches old age and starts to develop problems like incontinence and other health conditions that require the services of a vet their lovely pet now becomes a nuisance. I quickly remind them that like us humans animals also deserve the very best love and care in old age as a reward for the friendship that animal have given its owner throughout its life. These stories cause me great pain and only remind me that the human race can be incredibly cruel to its animal friends. I Once had a lady come to me and during the sitting she mentioned that her daughter had brought her a dog for Christmas and she did not really want another dog at her age, this is not a good idea I told her for someone else to decide whether or not you need a dog or come to mention it any other type pet, these animals like humans can sense they were not really wanted. Giving pets at Christmas time is in my opinion not a good idea, they may look cute and cuddly on Christmas day but in most cases the novelty soon evaporates and sometimes as the dog gets older its no longer wanted, a dog is not a present it should be something that has had a lot of research put in before hand so you have gained all the knowledge required on how to look after it and its needs. I find the statement a dog is for life not just for Christmas most apt and maybe it is time for breeders to stop selling them at this time of year.

There is one lovely old lady that passes our house everyday with her dog you always see the dog first on its long lead then she appears behind it.

She is getting slower these days but one day as we chatted over the front gate she told me she had always wanted a dog but her now deceased husband wouldn't let her have one, I have never been so happy she said he is so much company for me and gets me out of the house, its makes me so glad to see them both wandering past the house how wonderful animals can be for us humans in some cases life savers.

There is a lot to be said for some dog breeders in this country who are doing it purely for financial gain and not asking the right questions of potential dog owners, and recently we have the celebrity breeds labradoodles etc which fetch extortionate prices and become a must have status symbol rather than wanting a dog for love. You only have to look at this countries recent figures showing a increase in unwanted animals and cruelty yet we still breed more and more exotic species for human vanity. Maybe its time for more licensing in this country to protect the legitimate breeders and stop some of the home breeders who breed only for financial gain, maybe tagging all puppies sold should be made law. This may sound as a personal gripe but as a working medium I know what animals sense and think and the hurt they are going through.

Dogs need a lot of hard work put in and require human contact and the freedom to run not to be shut in a house or flat all day because the owners work. I always tell my clients to ask themselves these questions before they acquire a dog,

1) Are you at home all day.

2) Can you afford to pay the vet bills if the dog becomes sick.

3) Are you prepared to put in the hard work required when they are puppies.

4) Will you put your pet first before yourself.

5) Have you done your research, then you are ready.

The end of my person gripes so now on a lighter note the recent snows have given my dogs a wonderful experience, my little terrier is always eager to tear around the garden so I opened the back door for him thinking to myself what's he going to make of the snow, I stood back and watched as he sped round the corner as usual and suddenly as he reached the top of the steps he put on the brakes and looked behind him I knew he was thinking what's this white stuff then. It was so funny watching him creep down the steps one by one until he reached the snow and then sniffing it I could sense him thinking what do i do then eat it, run away or tell it off, it was a while before he gained the confidence to step on to the snow and before long he sped off the snow kicking up behind him he was having such fun and it made me so happy.

The next day he went out again and remembering the fun he had experienced the day before he sped down the steps but to his horror it had turned to ice and the crunching under his paws made him run in with his tail between his legs, it was not until the next day before things were back to normal and he could once again visit his territory. One of my other dogs a Shih Tzu called Sweep is like clockwork when it comes to meal times if I am a minute late he gives me the glare and nudges my leg until I get up I know he is thinking if you think you're sitting there any longer you're mistaken and this carries on until I feed him. He is such a greedy dog and was the biggest of the puppies when we got him he fed well off his mother I am sure, he has such a good temperament and the most balanced of all my other dogs, so laid back but the leader of the pack when its needed. He is a very precious dog, as in Vietnam the black and white Shih Tzu with a white lock of hair on the head and white paws are most popular because to have ones head and feet in the snow is a symbol of happiness. My dog Sweep has certainly been in the snow and brings me great happiness everyday. My other Shih Tzu called Teddy certainly fits into the origins and characters of the Shih Tzu Kou which can be traced back from the temples of Lhasa to the Imperial Court of China and known as the Tibetan lion dog because of its golden colour which was reminiscent of the symbolic lion of Tibet. The name was later modified, losing the Kou part and simply becoming Shih Tzu (Tibetan lion) retaining the image of the lion the symbolic mount of Budda, Teddy certainly shows these royal traits a very proud and noble dog, but a very loyal friend. All animals have their different characteristics and we can learn so much from them, they reward us for our kindness and are always there no matter what mood we may be in, a truly wonderful species.

I leave you with a final thought, keep looking, keep focused and always strive for the answers to your questions. I hope all my friends enjoy this read as have my guides and I, and we lave you with our love and hope you all achieve your desires and reach your goals in life.

Judith.

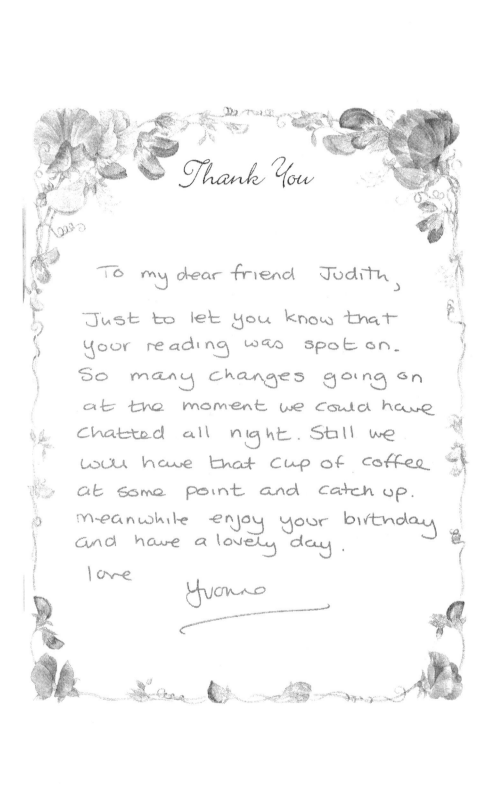

Thank You

To my dear friend Judith,

Just to let you know that
your reading was spot on.
So many changes going on
at the moment we could have
chatted all night. Still we
will have that cup of coffee
at some point and catch up.
meanwhile enjoy your birthday
and have a lovely day.

love

Yvonne

6/5/97

Thank You

Dear Judith,
    Thankyou ever so much
for the lovely spiritual reading
you gave me today — and I'm
sorry I was so tearful. I had
no idea that I'd be in tears.
But you put so much of yourself
into your readings and so
much love comes across.

Thank you ever so much for
helping me Judith.

God Bless + take care
        love Helena
            x

Judith,

Thank you very much indeed for my session yesterday (wh... you read this) you have a lovely Thanks, a very pleasant and calm manner.

Without my asking you have answered so many questions and eased my mind. You have a wonderful gift and use it so helpfully. I'm sure that your notes will help guide me on my journey. I do hope we meet up again sometime.

My very best wishes to you. Alan

Judith,

Thank you so much for all your help. I don't think you realize how much good you do and just how many lives you touch.

I really appreciate your patience and kindness.

Again many thanks,

take care

Mani

I forgot to ask how long I would be in my current job, oh well, a least it will give us something to talk about next time.

Dear Judith,

You have a great warmth & calmness about yourself which is a gift in itself.
I give thanks that in my desperation I found you,

When I was so low - you gave me hope,
When I was afraid - you gave me peace,
When I was alone - you showed me that I was not, I was surrounded by love & carers.

I will treasure this experiance and will treat it as a stepping stone towards my Journey in the future.

love
Carole
x

Lightning Source UK Ltd.
Milton Keynes UK
09 December 2009

147291UK00002B/74/P